Tales from the Crib

By Tammy Lee Garrison

Illustrated by
Stephanie Ann Miller

This is a work of fiction. All of the characters, organizations, and events portrayed in this book are either products of the author's imagination or are used fictionally.

Tales from the Crib

Copyright © 2018 by Tammy Garrison

All rights reserved. No part of this book may be used or reproduced in any manner whatsoever without written permission except in the case of brief quotations embodied in critical articles or reviews. For information address: Tammy Garrison 1182 S. Water Street, Silverton, OR 97381

Printed in the United States of America

Written and Dedicated to

Jayce Walker Garrison

Note:

These poems were written in song.

Make up your own tune and sing along.

Rise and Shine Song

Good morning. Good morning. Good morning to you.
Good morning, little baby. I love you.

Breakfast Song

Breakfast, breakfast, the most important time of the day.

Breakfast, breakfast, you better do what I say.

Breakfast, breakfast, it makes you strong so you can play!

Breakfast, breakfast, I eat it every day.

Breakfast. Yay!

Bath Time

(Point out each area)

Chest, stomach, legs, feet and toes.

Your arms, your hands, fingers and your nose.

Your head, your ears, that beautiful smile, too!

The back, the butt. Pee ewe!

But the most important part is to remember

that your mama loves you!

(Additional if you want)

What? Even if I fart? (fart noise)

Yes, even if you fart.

Mama loves you with all of her heart.

Banana Song

MMM. Banana.

MMM. MMM. Banana.

MMM Banana.

MMM MMM Banana.

BA NA NAH!

Sweet Potato

Sweet potato. Sweet potato. Sweet potato pie.

Sweet potato. Sweet potato.

Oh my my!

Sunday Football

Football! Football! I wanna play.

Football. Football. It's Sunday!

Games on all day long. Daddy's in the kitchen singing his song.

Football! Football!

All day long.

Daddy's in the Kitchen

I smell bacon in my nose.

Daddy's in the kitchen.

Oh no no.

I smell bacon in my nose nose nose.

Here comes Daddy!

Bacon, eggs, and potatoes!

Whoa!

Good Night Sweetheart

Good night sweetheart it's time to go.

Good night sweet heart it's time to go.

Badum Badum

Gonight sweetheart it's time to go.

Gonight sweetheart it's time to go.

To bed. To bed. (deep voice)

To bed I said.

(repeat)

Sleep my Angel

Go to sleep. Go to sleep.

Go to sleep my little baby.

Go to sleep.

Go to sleep. Go to sleeeeeep.

For tomorrow's a new day.

We will go out and play.

For tomorrow's a new day and we want to play.

(Repeat)

Acknowledgements

A special thanks to Lee Shaw for helping me make a dream come true.

A special thanks to my father for helping me come up with the title.

And a special thanks to my husband and family!

Author's Bio

With a musical heritage, Tammy Lee Garrison found it natural to sing little songs to her son throughout the day. In time, she wanted to make the little tunes available to others.

Tammy lives in Silverton, Oregon with her husband and son.

Made in the USA
San Bernardino, CA
07 June 2018